Who Is
Jackie Chan?

by Jody Jensen Shaffer

illustrated by Gregory Copeland

Penguin Workshop

For everyone who never gives up—JJS

For R.W.C, the IV—GC

PENGUIN WORKSHOP
An Imprint of Penguin Random House LLC, New York

Visit us online at www.penguinrandomhouse.com.

Library of Congress Control Number: 2019034725

ISBN 9781524791629 (paperback)   10 9 8 7 6 5 4 3 2 1
ISBN 9781524791636 (library binding)   10 9 8 7 6 5 4 3 2 1

Contents

Who Is Jackie Chan?

Seven-year-old Chan Kong-sang stared at his father. He could hardly believe it. They were going on a trip! His father had never taken him on a trip before. And especially not on a day when Kong-sang was supposed to be in school. He wasn't good at school, and he didn't like it. He got in trouble for being too active and not doing his work.

Kong-sang ran to his bedroom and put on his favorite outfit—a Western cowboy costume with a big hat and a plastic gun. It was his birthday gift from his parents. He waved to his mother and boarded the bus with his father.

"Where are we going?" he asked.

"Somewhere special," his father said.

They rode the bus down the mountain from his home on Victoria Peak, Hong Kong, to the city at the bottom. Kong-sang had never been to the city before. It was filled with unfamiliar sounds and smells. But he did recognize one thing: sweet buns! The flaky sweet rolls were the boy's favorite. He begged his father to buy a bag of the steaming treats.

Delicious sweet buns in hand, Kong-sang and his father boarded a ferry, another new experience for the boy. They chugged across Victoria Harbour toward the bustling city of Kowloon. Kong-sang and his father pushed through the crowd, past cars, buildings, and signs advertising food and music. Then they turned onto a street lined with old apartment buildings. Kong-sang's heart sank. There was nothing exciting here. Was their adventure over?

They stopped in front of a building with a sign that read China Drama Academy. "Here we are," said his father. As the doors opened and Kong-sang saw inside, his heart raced. Boys and girls in black-and-white outfits kicked

and jumped, somersaulted, and tumbled. Kong-sang was in heaven! It was a school to learn how to perform martial arts. And that was the kind of school an active boy like Kong-sang could love.

CHAPTER 1
Early Years

Chan Kong-sang was born on April 7, 1954, on Victoria Peak—the highest mountain in Hong Kong. His parents were called Charles and Lee-Lee. Kong-sang was a big baby. He weighed twelve pounds! Kong-sang was so big and heavy that his parents nicknamed him "Pao-pao." It means *cannonball* in Chinese.

Kong-sang's parents were very poor. His mother was a housekeeper. His father was a cook. The couple worked for the French ambassador to Hong Kong. The ambassador was a diplomat who was sent to represent France in the region. He lived with his family in a large house in Hong Kong. Kong-sang's family lived in a tiny room with no windows at the back of the ambassador's mansion.

As a four- or five-year-old, Kong-sang exercised every day. His father woke him early in the morning to work out. Kong-sang's father came from Shandong Province, China, where martial arts were very popular. Martial arts are fighting traditions for self-defense and combat, but they are also used for health and fitness. In Shandong, the people especially liked a kind of martial arts called Northern style kung fu. It focused on spinning kicks and acrobatic movements.

China and Hong Kong

From 1945 to 1949, China fought a civil war that split the country into two sides. On one side was the Communist Party of China. On the other was the Nationalist Party. The Communist Party won the war. They founded the People's Republic of China.

During this same time, the territory of Hong Kong was ruled by the United Kingdom. Its governor was appointed by Parliament in London, England. Hong Kong had become one of the most important financial centers and trading ports in the world.

In July 1997, the United Kingdom returned rule of Hong Kong to the Chinese government. But even today, Hong Kong still has its own money, Olympic team, flag, and legal system.

Kong-sang and his father didn't have a gym. So they used extra pieces of wood and recycled trash for equipment. They ran, lifted sandbags, and did push-ups. To Kong-sang's father, learning the Northern style of kung fu was very important. It was the same thing as learning how to become a man.

When Kong-sang was six, his parents sent
him to school at Nan Hua Elementary Academy.
Kong-sang did not like it. He had trouble reading
and understanding the teacher. He didn't do
his homework. He didn't like staying indoors.
And he was bored. Kong-sang became a class
clown. He got in trouble with his teachers.

What Are Martial Arts?

Martial arts are forms of combat and self-defense. They are mostly used as sport. Martial arts include karate, kung fu, judo, tae kwon do, and jujitsu. There is overlap among the types of martial arts, but each one has a different focus. Karate uses kicks and punches delivered with special shouts. Judo is like wrestling.

Jujitsu uses holds and blocks. Kung fu focuses on low stances and powerful blocks.

Originally, kung fu was based on the fighting styles of five animals: tiger, crane, leopard, snake, and dragon. People practice two styles of kung fu: Northern style and Southern style. Northern style is acrobatic. It uses flashy, spinning kicks. Southern style uses strong defensive postures and powerful fist techniques.

And sometimes he got into fights with other kids in his neighborhood.

When Kong-sang's parents learned their son would have to repeat his first year, they took him out of school. Around this same time, Kong-sang's father was offered a better job in Australia. He was going to be a cook at the US embassy there. But that would mean leaving his family and moving far away. Seven-year-old Kong-sang seemed too wild for his mother to handle by herself at home. His parents wondered if the China Drama Academy in nearby Kowloon, Hong Kong, might be a good place for their son.

The China Drama Academy was one of the Peking Opera schools. At the China Drama Academy, students learned discipline and martial arts so they could perform in the Chinese opera. The Chans decided to find out more about the academy.

The Chinese Opera

The Chinese opera began over a thousand years ago. Early performances were simple plays involving just two actors. Over time, more actors and more complex plots were introduced.

In modern times, the Chinese opera combined gymnastics, acting, singing, and stage combat. Students who performed in the Chinese opera frequently lived together at their schools. They rehearsed, ate, and slept together. They usually lived at the school for seven or ten years. School leaders were very strict. They frequently punished students who made mistakes. Students performed for their communities to raise money for their schools. Students also studied traditional subjects like writing and history, but they spent most of their time perfecting the art of performance. Most of the students hoped to have movie careers as stuntmen and stuntwomen after they graduated.

CHAPTER 2
The China Drama Academy

One day, Kong-sang's father told him they were taking a trip: They were going to Kowloon. Kong-sang was very excited. He put on his favorite cowboy costume. When they got to the China Drama Academy, Kong-sang had no idea where they were. But as soon as the door opened, he became very curious about what he found there.

In a large, open room, Kong-sang saw twenty boys and girls in black-and-white outfits. They performed martial arts routines. They staged pretend battles with swords and sticks. They practiced somersaults. Kong-sang was thrilled! His father spoke with Master Yu Jim-yuen, who was in charge of the school, while Kong-sang joined the other children.

Master Yu Jim-yuen

Together they kicked, swung weapons, and practiced stances. Most of the students were kind to Kong-sang, teaching him small things and laughing with him when he made a mistake. But one older student had a warning for him: "Listen, cowboy, you may think this is all fun and games. But this is what we *eat, drink, and dream.* This is our *lives.*" Despite such serious words, Kong-sang loved his visit to the academy.

The Chans returned to the academy two more times. After each visit, Kong-sang's parents asked their son if he liked this new school. He did. Then one day, they packed a suitcase for Kong-sang. It was time for his father to leave for Australia, and he would be away for a long time. Kong-sang's mother would continue to work at the ambassador's house in Victoria Peak.

And Kong-sang would live at the China Drama Academy.

Kong-sang was happy! He thought that meant he wouldn't have to go to school or do chores. The only question was how long he wanted to stay at the academy. Kong-sang told his parents he wanted to stay forever! His parents signed a contract for ten years. Kong-sang was only seven years old. He would live at the academy until he was a teenager.

Kong-sang quickly learned that life at the academy was not what it had seemed. There was a strict order there. Master Yu was at the top. Yuen Lung, the student who warned Kong-sang on his first visit, was next. He was the oldest student and was called "Big Brother." Kong-sang had to call everyone older than himself Big Brother or Big Sister. The older students were not always nice to the younger ones. Yuen Lung gave Kong-sang a mean nickname. He called him "Big Nose."

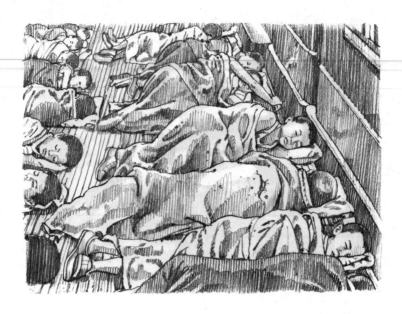

Life at the academy was hard. The students only got five hours of sleep each night. Kong-sang slept on the floor under a moth-eaten blanket. The students got up at 5:00 a.m. They trained for more than sixteen hours each day, seven days a week. They ran, marched, and learned flips, somersaults, and martial arts. "We would never take off the shoes," he later remembered. "You don't have time." Students practiced punching and kicking thousands of times each day.

After a small lunch of rice, vegetables, and fried fish, the students did splits and handstands for hours. Once practice was finished, they cleaned the kitchen or courtyard, or took singing lessons. Sometimes the students learned face painting, how to use props, and how to wear opera costumes.

Then it was time for the part Kong-sang was not so happy about—schoolwork. Students read, wrote, and studied Chinese history for a couple of hours after dinner each day.

It was a hard life. If a student misbehaved,

Master Yu hit him with a stick. Kong-sang only saw his mother once a week. She carried hot water from her home on Victoria Peak all the way to the academy in Kowloon. She wanted to make sure Kong-sang had at least one bath a week.

Kong-sang got his first real look at a professional opera on a school trip. From his seat in the audience, he saw the theater curtains part and the actors whirl in a grand battle. He was thrilled! He hoped that someday all his hard work and training would lead to something like that. "I wanted to hear a crowd clapping and cheering and screaming for *me*." It was hard work, but Kong-sang was an excellent kung fu student. He could do acrobatics, sing, and perform martial arts.

He was chosen as one of the "Seven Little Fortunes"—a special performing group within the China Drama Academy. Kong-sang played small roles at first. But soon he starred in a few performances. Sometimes Master Yu let students audition for movie roles outside the academy. Kong-sang was one of those students. When he was only eight years old, he played an extra in the film *Big and Little Wong Tin Bar*.

Then one day when Kong-sang was nine years old, Master Yu announced that Kong-sang's parents were coming for a visit. Kong-sang hadn't seen his father for years and had only communicated with him through letters. He worried his parents were going to take him out of the academy. What else could be important enough that his father would make a trip home from Australia?

At one time in his young life, Kong-sang had wanted to be a lawyer, an engineer, or a doctor. But since he wasn't a great student, he had fallen in love with the opera. Now he couldn't imagine doing anything else. He wondered what his parents could have in mind.

But Kong-sang's parents hadn't come to take him away. That night, over dinner with the entire academy, they told him that his mother was moving to Australia to be with his father. They didn't want Kong-sang to leave the academy,

but they also knew he needed an adult who lived close by. They wanted Master Yu to adopt Kong-sang as his godson!

Kong-sang was sad to know that his mother was leaving the country. But he was happy about staying at the academy. He thought it was a great honor to be adopted by his master. He only learned later how difficult that would be. Now Kong-sang had to be an example for the other students. So when someone got punished, Kong-sang was punished twice as much.

Hong Kong Cinema

The word *cinema* refers to both the movies and the art of making them. Hong Kong cinema is one of the largest motion picture industries in the world. It combines mythical storytelling and kung fu action. Hong Kong cinema began in the 1920s in Shanghai, China. Films from that time were set in ancient China. They featured magical creatures like beasts and spirits. But the Chinese government didn't like the films. They thought these kinds of stories made

people superstitious. The government banned the films. But movie companies still wanted to make them. So the Shanghai film companies moved to Hong Kong, where Chinese laws didn't apply.

Once in Hong Kong, the studios kept making films with magical elements. But they added more realistic kung fu elements, too.

In the 1970s, Bruce Lee began making martial arts movies in Hong Kong. He became a superstar. And Hong Kong cinema became popular with an international audience.

Bruce Lee in *The Big Boss*

Eventually, audiences for the live performances of the Chinese opera shrank. People preferred going to the movies—especially to see martial arts films. No new students were entering the academy. Master Yu let more and more of his students perform as extras on movie sets. Kong-sang sometimes performed stunts for the Shaw Brothers movie studio.

Shaw Brothers studio logo

When he turned seventeen, Kong-sang's time at the academy came to an end. His father picked him up from the place where he'd spent most of his childhood. Kong-sang shouted for joy when the car pulled away! He had liked many things about the academy. But there were lots of things he hadn't liked, too. He was ready to be on his own.

CHAPTER 3
On His Own

After Kong-sang graduated from the academy, his parents wanted him to move to Australia with them. His father knew people who could help Kong-sang get a job. But he told his parents he had a contract to work as a movie stuntman in Hong Kong. It wasn't true. But Kong-sang was too embarrassed to tell his parents he didn't have

a job. His parents bought him an apartment in Hong Kong. He was so poor he made tables and chairs from scrap pieces of wood he found in the streets.

What Is a Stuntperson?

A stuntperson is a trained professional who stages dangerous scenes—like falls, jumps, tumbles, fights, and car crashes—in place of another actor, often the film's star. Stuntmen and stuntwomen—sometimes known as "stunt doubles"—take on the most risky action work on a film or television set.

Kong-sang went to the Shaw Brothers movie studio every day to look for work. He waited in line with all the other out-of-work stuntpeople listening for their names to be called.

Often Kong-sang acted as a stunt double for the star of a movie. A studio couldn't afford to let its star get hurt. So skilled performers like Kong-sang did the diving, jumping, punching, and kicking for them. He worked from sunup to sundown, and he got better and better at what he did.

Slowly, Kong-sang moved up the ranks of the stunt crew. He was asked to perform real, and dangerous, stunts. His schoolmate from the academy, Yuen Lung (who now went by the name Sammo Hung) helped him find even more work. Kong-sang rose to the top of his profession. In a very short time, he had become a respected stuntman doing very risky stunts. But he wasn't a movie star. And he really wanted to become one.

Sammo Hung

In 1971, Bruce Lee began making films in Hong Kong. Lee was a Chinese actor and martial artist who had been born in the United States. He changed the Hong Kong film industry forever. Instead of using the traditional,

stiff style of combat of the classic martial arts movies, Lee played street fighters and tough guys. Chinese audiences loved it. Movie studios rushed to sign actors who looked, talked, and fought like Bruce Lee.

Bruce Lee (1940–1973)

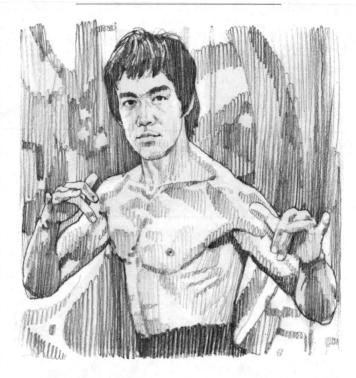

Bruce Lee was born Li Jun Fan in San Francisco, California, in 1940. His family moved to Hong Kong when Lee was still a baby. At age eighteen, Lee moved back to San Francisco. He went to college and eventually opened a kung fu school.

During a visit to Hong Kong, the producer Raymond Chow asked Lee to star in a movie called *The Big Boss*. It was a hit with Chinese audiences. Bruce Lee went on to star in movies such as *Fist of Fury*, *The Way of the Dragon*, and *Enter the Dragon*.

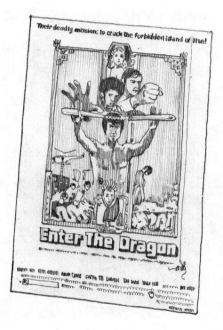

He became an international superstar and one of the biggest martial arts actors in history.

Kong-sang wondered if he could ever be as famous as Bruce Lee. He certainly wanted to try. When he was offered a stunt job on Lee's movie *Fist of Fury*, he was thrilled. He was asked to do some very dangerous stunts. For one, Kong-sang would have to launch himself backward, get pulled through a door by wires, and then fall from twenty feet off the ground into a roll—

all in one scene! Kong-sang performed the dangerous stunt perfectly, but he was knocked unconscious toward the end. When he awoke, Bruce Lee was standing over him. "Very good," he said. "That's a print." Bruce meant that the scene was so good, it would be the perfect shot to use in the movie, the one that would get printed on the actual film.

Kong-sang learned from his experience on *Fist of Fury* that he no longer wanted to be just a stuntman. He wanted to be a stunt coordinator—the person who designs the flow of the action and who tells other stuntpeople what to do. He believed he could become the youngest stunt coordinator in Hong Kong. "When I put my mind to it, I feel like I can do just about anything." Kong-sang got his wish, and he began coordinating stunts for many movies in Hong Kong.

Then the unthinkable happened. In July 1973, Bruce Lee suddenly died. Movie-studio executives tried to find "the next Bruce Lee." But

no one could replace the superstar. Attendance at martial arts movies dropped. Kong-sang's stunt work slowed, too. As a stuntman, he had not been considered an actor. He didn't have any lines to speak, and he was used only during action scenes. But he wanted to become an action-movie star and not just a stuntman or stunt coordinator. When martial arts movies became less popular after Lee's death, Kong-sang worried that his dream of becoming a star would never come true.

But then Kong-sang was offered a small, supporting role in a movie called *Hand of Death*. He wasn't the star, but this was a start. On the set, Kong-sang learned many things about acting. He even learned some things about directing. But Bruce Lee's death had hurt the movie studios too much. After *Hand of Death*, they didn't have many new opportunities for Kong-sang. Heartbroken, he decided to move to Australia and live with his parents after all.

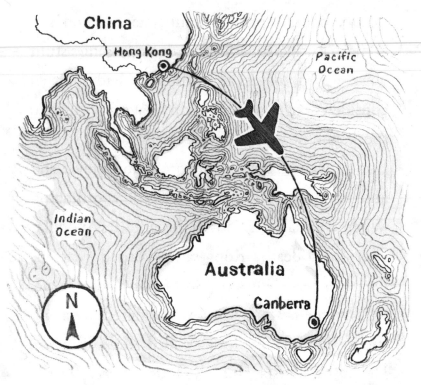

After arriving in Canberra, Australia, in 1976, Kong-sang enrolled in English classes. He had never learned English, and that is the language Australians speak. He tried hard at school. But Kong-sang "couldn't even get past the ABCs." He quit school again and began working at a construction job.

He moved bricks around a building site in the hot sun. Kong-sang's boss was named Jack. When he introduced Kong-sang to the other workers, he pointed at him and said, "His name's Jack, too." His coworkers called him Little Jack. Kong-sang later added -*ie* to his name. From then on, he was known as "Jackie Chan."

Jackie took a second job at night chopping vegetables in a Chinese restaurant. With two jobs, he was very busy. But he wasn't happy, and his mom could tell. She suggested Jackie go back to Hong Kong and follow his dream to become an actor.

"You were born to be a great man, and you will go on to do great things. But you can't do them here. This is not where you belong."

Later that same year, Jackie got a telegram from Willie Chan, the general manager for Lo Wei Motion Picture Company back in Hong Kong. The studio was going to remake Bruce Lee's *Fist of Fury*, and they wanted Jackie to play the lead role, the role Bruce Lee had played! Jackie would be paid about $350 a month—much more money than he had ever earned before! He moved back to Hong Kong right away and signed a contract.

Jackie agreed to act for Lo Wei Motion Picture Company for eight years. During that time he'd have to make any movie they decided to put him in. But Jackie didn't mind. At least he'd be acting!

CHAPTER 4
Kung Fu Comedy

Jackie was back in Hong Kong with a bright future ahead of him. He starred in *New Fist of Fury*, and he was also the stunt coordinator for the film. But there was something wrong. Jackie found his own acting stiff and unnatural. The director wanted him to be fierce, just like Bruce Lee had been. But that was not Jackie's style. He wanted to be less violent and sometimes even funny.

In his next several films, Jackie tried acting more playful and sillier. He made funny faces and told jokes when things didn't go well for his characters. But the studio didn't like Jackie's original comedy. And Jackie had to do what Lo Wei Motion Picture Company wanted.

Two years passed. Jackie starred in a few
movies that didn't do very well. Then he wrote
and starred in a funny movie that was much
more his style. *Half a Loaf of Kung Fu* was about
an acrobat who wanted to be a bodyguard.

Jackie had loved watching older silent movies with stars like Charlie Chaplin and Buster Keaton. They worked dangerous stunts into funny scenes—exactly the way Jackie wanted to.

But *Half a Loaf of Kung Fu* was not released until much later. The director didn't like how the film had turned out. Jackie was *very* unhappy. He asked to be loaned to another studio for

a while. Jackie hoped the new studio would let him star in the kind of movies he wanted to make.

Things started off great at Seasonal Films. Jackie told his bosses at the new studio to reconsider trying to create the next Bruce Lee. He thought they should try to be "Bruce's opposite. Bruce kicked very high . . . I say we should kick as low to the ground as possible. Bruce screamed when he hit someone to show his strength and anger. I say we should scream to show how much hitting someone hurts your hand . . . Bruce was Superman, but I think audiences want to see someone who's just a man.

Like them. Someone who wins only after making a lot of mistakes, who has a sense of humor." In his next film, Jackie got a chance to make the kind of movie he wanted to make.

In *Snake in Eagle's Shadow*, Jackie reinvented the

Snake in Eagle's Shadow movie poster

martial arts movie. He turned the traditional roles of master and student upside down. Instead of the master of the school being a powerful expert in martial arts, he would be less talented than the student. Instead of the student being clumsy and inexperienced, he would be the hero. The student would learn real martial arts from an old man on the street.

Snake in Eagle's Shadow was a blockbuster hit!

Jackie's Favorite Funnymen

The very first movies made in the late 1800s and early 1900s were called "moving pictures." They had images but no sound. Buster Keaton, Charlie Chaplin, and Harold Lloyd were some of the biggest silent-film stars. Jackie loved the comedy and action of all three.

Charlie Chaplin (1889– 1977) was one of the first truly great film stars. His most famous character was called "the Tramp." He had baggy pants and a funny mustache. Chaplin was an actor and a comedian. Some of his

Charlie Chaplin

films—*The Kid*, *The Gold Rush*, and *City Lights*—are considered classics.

Buster Keaton

Joseph Frank "Buster" Keaton (1895–1966) grew up with parents who were stage actors. "The Three Keatons" were known for their physical tricks and dangerous stunts onstage. *The General* is one of Keaton's most well-known movies. His nickname was "the Great Stone Face."

Harold Lloyd's (1893–1971) first comedy character was a copy of Chaplin's Tramp. Lloyd soon made famous his own ambitious, glasses-wearing character, sometimes referred to as "Glasses." One of Lloyd's most memorable and dangerous scenes was when he hung from a clock in the movie *Safety Last!*

Harold Lloyd

It earned even more money in Hong Kong than Bruce Lee's *Fist of Fury*. Jackie couldn't believe it. He wasn't sure "poor, uneducated, unhandsome boys" like him could become stars. Now he knew better. His next movie, *Drunken Master*, was so successful that it made Jackie a celebrity all over Asia.

For the first time, people recognized Jackie in public. They asked for interviews and autographs. He was making more money than he ever had. He bought himself an expensive watch for each day of the week and expensive gifts for his parents, too.

Jackie went back to Lo Wei Motion Picture Company. He starred in and, for the first time, directed a film, *The Fearless Hyena*. It was more

successful than his previous hits. Even more studios wanted to work with Jackie. Golden Harvest offered him nearly half a million dollars to work for them! They also offered him a chance to make movies in America.

Jackie was excited. He wondered if he could be a star in the United States, too.

CHAPTER 5
Dangerous Stunts and Near Misses

Jackie's first trip to the United States was to star in the movie *Battle Creek Brawl*, which would be filmed in Texas. It was about a young man who is warned not to show his kung fu skills until one day he is forced to. But life in Texas was hard. Jackie knew very little English. He had a difficult time even ordering breakfast.

Sometimes he called his manager, Willie Chan, in Hong Kong to translate his order for him! And he had to learn all his English lines in just two weeks. A tutor helped him during the day, and he watched TV at night to listen to English words.

But when filming began, Jackie was unhappy. American filmmaking was different than Hong Kong cinema. It was much more planned, with every scene written and sketched out in advance. He felt it left little room for creativity. When the movie, now called *The Big Brawl*, finished filming, Jackie couldn't wait to get back to Hong Kong. But Golden Harvest had other plans. They sent Jackie on a tour of California to promote the movie instead.

Jackie was not happy. He had trouble answering reporters' questions. They confused kung fu with karate, and they asked if he was the next Bruce Lee. Jackie decided he didn't need to be a star in America. He was a star in Asia.

Even though *The Big Brawl* was not a success,
Golden Harvest wanted him to make another

movie. They hoped *The Cannonball Run* would earn more money. The movie was a big hit— for all the other actors. But it didn't show off Jackie's martial arts skills and talent. He played a race-car driver, so he was sitting for most of his scenes. "Nobody knew who this little Chinese guy was that spoke no English," Jackie said later.

Discouraged, Jackie went back to Hong Kong. He was ready to make movies the way he wanted. He starred in *Project A* in 1983. It was a huge success. For the first time, Jackie had done something his films have come to be known for: a really dangerous stunt. Jackie hung from a clock tower and fell fifty feet through two cloth awnings before he hit the ground. He did the stunt three times. He wanted the cameras to get the right angles.

Jackie never used special effects or stunt doubles for his work. "No blue screens and computer special effects. No stunt doubles. Real action. Real danger. And sometimes, real and terrible injury," Jackie wrote. Jackie was scared the entire time he did such dangerous stunts. "Anyone who really thinks I'm not scared out of my wits when I'm about to do one of these stunts is nuttier than I am."

Jackie began dating a Taiwanese actress named Lin Feng-jiao around this time. They were married in 1982 and had a son, Jaycee.

Jackie was the biggest movie star in Asia now, even though American audiences were mostly unaware of him.

Jackie continued to make hit movies in Hong Kong. In 1986, he started a production company there called Golden Way Films. A production company chooses which films to make, hires actors, and shoots and releases movies.

He also began a modeling agency and an organization to help stuntpeople pay for doctor visits. Too many had been hurt while filming the movie *Police Story*. Like Jackie had experienced earlier, they sometimes had trouble paying their doctors for medical care. Jackie helped them because he knew just how dangerous stunt work could be.

Jackie's Spectacular Stunts

Jackie has performed many amazing stunts over the course of his career, including:

- Using the handle of an umbrella to grab an open bus window and being thrown onto the highway below

- Driving a car down a mountainside, zigzagging through, not around, buildings in the village

- Sliding down the side of a twenty-one-story building

- Running along the tops of moving buses while dodging signs and billboards overhead

- Parachuting from a plane to appear to jump over a cliff, landing on top of a hot-air balloon

- Roller-skating *over* a Volkswagen Beetle and then *under* an eighteen-wheeler truck

In fact, in 1986, Jackie was seriously hurt. He was in Yugoslavia filming a movie called *Armour of God* when an easy stunt went wrong. He was supposed to jump from the top of a building to a tree. But the tree branches broke, and Jackie fell to the ground. He hit his head on a rock and was rushed to the hospital.

Fortunately, doctors were able to operate quickly. He was grateful the doctors did a good job fixing such a difficult injury.

For the next ten years, Jackie continued to make and star in action movies in Hong Kong. Most were hits. Jackie became an even bigger star in other Asian countries and throughout the world. But he was still waiting to become an American movie star.

CHAPTER 6
Jackie in Hollywood

Jackie was forty-one years old by 1995. He wasn't able to do all the dangerous stunts he had when he was younger. Fights and stunts took him longer. He had never used special effects or stunt doubles before in his movies. But his longtime manager, Willie Chan, asked him to consider it.

Around this time, Jackie decided to give Hollywood another try. After all, he still had two dreams: a "big, glitzy, gala opening-night premiere, with photographers and velvet ropes and celebrities, just like on TV . . . [and] to get my hands and name printed in the cement outside the famous Mann's Chinese Theatre in Hollywood." Mann's was originally called Grauman's Chinese Theatre. Many famous people have left their handprints and footprints in cement there. So Jackie began looking for the right script for an American movie.

Jackie found just the film he was dreaming of in 1995's *Rumble in the Bronx.* It was risky filming some of the more dangerous scenes. One required Jackie to jump from a bridge to a moving hovercraft. When Jackie landed on a boat, he fell backward and twisted his right foot. He was hospitalized and used a wheelchair for weeks.

Jackie had been in over one hundred films by this time, but he had finally found the movie that made him a star in the United States! *Rumble in the Bronx* became the first Hong Kong film ever to make it to number one at the US box office. Jackie's next American movie  did even better. It made him a truly international celebrity.

In 1998, American director Brett Ratner asked Jackie if he'd like to star in a buddy-cop movie. He would play a Chinese police officer, and comedian Chris Tucker would play a Los Angeles policeman. Jackie agreed, but after he met his costar, neither actor was sure it was a good idea. Chris Tucker was surprised to learn that Jackie's English wasn't very good.

Grauman's Chinese Theatre

Grauman's Chinese Theatre opened in Hollywood, California, on May 18, 1927. Fans along Hollywood Boulevard waited to see movie stars and celebrities as they entered the theater for the premiere of a movie called *The King of Kings*.

Since that time, Grauman's Chinese Theatre on the historic Hollywood Walk of Fame has been the site of many movie openings. Fans gather to see famous actors and actresses arrive and walk up the red carpet into the theater. Movie stars are sometimes asked to leave their handprints and footprints, and sometimes their leg or nose prints, in cement near the entrance of the theater in an area known as the Forecourt of the Stars.

More than five million visitors from all over the world go to the theater each year to watch a movie, see the stars' handprints, or tour the famous venue. From 1973 to 2001 it was renamed Mann's Chinese Theatre, then reverted to its original name until 2013, when it became TCL Chinese Theatre.

And Jackie was concerned that he couldn't understand Chris. But the director thought they would be great together.

As filming for *Rush Hour* finished, Jackie felt certain that the movie had not turned out well. He didn't understand what the audience was laughing at during the movie's premiere. But audiences loved Jackie's kung fu

Chris Tucker

moves, his silly charm, and Chris Tucker's fast-talking energy. The two actors had grown to really like each other, and it showed on the screen.

Jackie was back at work in Hong Kong when he got word that *Rush Hour* was a huge hit in the United States. Audiences loved the movie so much, they stuck around to watch the outtakes—

scenes that were not included in the final movie—in the end credits. They thought those were even funnier. *Rush Hour* made more than $140 million in the United States alone and was one of the biggest moneymaking movies of 1998. Jackie finally had a successful Hollywood career for English-speaking audiences and a Hong Kong career for Chinese-speaking fans.

Buddy Films

American movies that pair two main characters together are sometimes called buddy films. These movies put two very different people in circumstances where they have to work together. In the end, they often find they need each other, and they end up being friends.

The two main types of buddy films are comedy and action films, or a combination of both.

In addition to *Rush Hour*, some examples of classic buddy films are *Dumb and Dumber*, *Men in Black*, *Shanghai Noon*, *Shanghai Knights*, and the Shrek movies that pair the title ogre with an irritating donkey who ends up becoming his best friend.

CHAPTER 7
Blockbuster Decade

Jackie's movie career in the United States took off over the next several years. In 2000, he starred in the buddy western *Shanghai Noon* with Owen Wilson and Lucy Liu. It was an international hit and made almost $100 million worldwide. Jackie and Chris Tucker teamed up for a second *Rush Hour* movie in 2001, and in 2002, Jackie received a star on the Hollywood Walk of Fame.

Lucy Liu (1968–)

Lucy Liu is an American actress, director, and producer. She was born in New York City on December 2, 1968. While attending college in Michigan, Liu auditioned for a supporting role in a production of *Alice in Wonderland*. She ended up getting the lead part and decided to try acting as a career.

She got her big break in 1997 when she was cast as Ling Woo in the television show *Ally McBeal*. Since then, Liu has starred in several movies and television shows, including *Shanghai Noon*, *Shanghai Knights*, *Charlie's Angels*, and *Elementary*. Liu also voices the character of Master Viper in the *Kung Fu Panda* movies.

That same year, *The Tuxedo*, with Jennifer Love Hewitt, hit theaters. Jackie, Owen Wilson, and Lucy Liu released a follow-up to *Shanghai Noon*, called *Shanghai Knights*, in 2003.

In 2004, Jackie starred in the movie *Around the World in 80 Days*, about a British inventor who travels around the globe. It was based on the 1873 novel by Jules Verne. In 2007, Jackie and Chris Tucker joined forces for another installment of their buddy-cop movies, *Rush Hour 3*. And in 2008, Jackie began voicing characters in animated movies. He was the voice of Master Monkey in *Kung Fu Panda* and its sequels.

Jackie became a master of a different kind in his next movie. In 2010, he starred in the remake of a classic American movie. He played a maintenance man, Mr. Han, in *The Karate Kid* with Jaden Smith. Jaden's parents,

actors Will Smith and Jada Pinkett Smith, produced the movie. When Will asked Jackie if he would be in the film, Jackie agreed right away. But he was confused. Jackie assumed *he* would be the kung fu student. He wondered who would play the master!

1984's *The Karate Kid*

Ralph Macchio and Pat Morita in *The Karate Kid*

The original *The Karate Kid* tells the story of a martial arts master who teaches karate to a bullied boy in the United States. It stars Ralph Macchio as the bullied kid and Pat Morita as the master. It was a huge hit in 1984, earning $90.8 million at the box office. Morita earned a Best Actor in a Supporting Role nomination at the 1985 Academy Awards for his work. The movie has had three sequels and an animated TV series.

Audiences loved the new *The Karate Kid* and the relationship between Mr. Han and Dre Parker, Jaden's character. The movie earned $359 million worldwide, and Jackie won a People's Choice Award in 2011 for playing Mr. Han.

In 2014, Jackie voiced a mouse in *The Nut Job*, and he starred as the voice of Master Wu/ Mister Liu in *The LEGO Ninjago Movie*, released in 2017.

Jackie is still acting, but since 2010, he mostly focuses on Chinese-language films. He has also been busy behind the scenes. In fact, Jackie holds the Guinness World Record for most credits on a single movie, fifteen! Jackie starred in, directed, wrote, produced, and even coordinated the catering for the film *Chinese Zodiac* in 2012. He was also the person in charge of the camera crew, the head electrician, and the art director!

And in 2013, Jackie left the imprint of his hands and feet in cement in front of Grauman's Chinese Theatre for the second time. Costars Chris Tucker and Jaden Smith were there to cheer him on.

Jackie also owns and operates the Jackie Chan International Stunt Training Base not far from his home in Beijing, China. He trains young people to do stunts the way he was taught, without doubles, computers, or computer-generated imagery (CGI). In the huge, state-of-the-art complex, Jackie's students tumble, leap,

spin, and box. They swing on ropes, practice with swords and wooden staffs, jump on trampolines, and practice taking falls.

CHAPTER 8
Jackie of All Trades

Jackie Chan is known throughout the world for martial arts movies with incredible stunts. But Jackie has many other interests and projects besides movies. He is a businessman in China, where he owns restaurants and theaters, coffee shops, and several clothing lines.

He has plans for a Jackie Chan theme park, where sets and props from his movies will be on display. And, believe it or not, Jackie is a pop star, too! He began recording songs in the 1980s and has made more than twenty full albums.

Jackie spends many hours volunteering with and raising money for causes that are important to him. Some of his most important work is done for others. He has been a UNICEF Goodwill Ambassador since 2004, giving hope to children who are poor or have illnesses like HIV.

Jackie supports children through the Jackie
Chan Charitable Foundation in Hong Kong.
And his Dragon's Heart Foundation helped
build more than twenty schools in China.

Because he wishes he had been a better student when he was in school, Jackie always promotes the importance of education.

Giving back hasn't always been so important

to Jackie. When he was first starting out in movies, he just wanted "to be famous and to earn more money." But now he likes helping others. "Even when I am sleeping, I think [about] how I can help other people. Every human being has to learn how to do charity."

In 2006, Jackie announced he will one day donate half his money to charity. He has donated millions of dollars and supplies to victims of earthquakes and droughts around the world. And in 2015, Jackie was named Singapore's first anti-drug ambassador.

Jackie Sings

In addition to singing on his own albums, Jackie has actually sung in a movie. When Disney's animated *Mulan* was released in China in 1998, it was Jackie who sang the theme song, "I'll Make a Man Out of You."

Jackie sang in two Chinese languages for the song: Mandarin and Cantonese. (Most people in Hong Kong speak Cantonese. Most people in China speak Mandarin.) He also provided the voice of Li Shang for all the Chinese-language versions of the film.

CHAPTER 9
Still Dreaming

Jackie has received many awards throughout his career. But the one that meant the most was the Academy Award he was given in 2016. He received an Honorary Oscar Award for lifetime achievement. "Standing here is a dream," Jackie said as he accepted his award. "After fifty-six years in the film industry, making more than two hundred films, breaking so many bones, finally this is mine." He never thought he would receive an Oscar for making action movies and comedies.

What's next for Jackie? Just like when he was a young boy at the China Drama Academy, he is still dreaming. He wants to make movies that people will remember for a long time.

From Martial Arts to Movie Sets

Besides Jackie Chan, the martial artists who have had the most successful acting careers are Jet Li, Chuck Norris, and Michelle Yeoh.

- Jet Li was born Li Lian-jie in Beijing, China, in 1963. He began learning wushu, a form of martial arts, when he was eight, and won the first of five gold medals by the age of eleven. He began acting in movies in 1982 when he starred in *The Shaolin Temple.* He has made both Chinese and Hollywood films since 1994, including *Lethal Weapon 4* in 1998, *Romeo Must Die* in 2000, and in 2010 *The Expendables* and its sequels.

- Chuck Norris was born in 1940 and grew up in California. After high school, he joined the air force and studied tang soo do, a Korean martial art. From 1964 to 1974, he won several martial arts championships before beginning his acting career. Norris is known for his roles in *Return of the Dragon*; *Walker, Texas Ranger*; and *Expendables 2*.

- Michelle Yeoh was born in 1962 in Ipoh, Malaysia. She moved to London to study ballet as a teenager. In 1985, she began making action movies. Never formally trained as a martial artist, she relied on movie trainers to help create her scenes. In 2000, she starred in *Crouching Tiger, Hidden Dragon*.

Jet Li, Chuck Norris, and Michelle Yeoh

He would like to act in a movie that isn't a comedy or one in which he doesn't throw any punches.

"I want to prove I'm a real actor. I'm not [just] an action star. If a director hires me to do a slow-motion [movie], singing a song, I'd like it!" He knows he'll have to keep changing to stay in the industry. Jackie's 2017 movie, *The Foreigner*, in which he plays a Chinese restaurant owner who is seeking revenge, was a step in a new direction.

What Jackie really wants after all these years is what almost every actor wants, a best actor Oscar. He understands that it's not easy to make the leap from action star to dramatic acting roles. But he's determined to give it a try.

Jackie has lived an extraordinary life. From the son of hardworking parents to Peking Opera student to international martial arts movie star and businessman, Jackie has done it all. But he has never forgotten all the effort his journey required.

He remembers when he was young and just starting out. While everyone else at the academy was sleeping, Jackie was practicing kung fu moves alone in front of a mirror. Jackie dreamed, worked hard, and believed in himself. That formula has been his perfect one-two punch for success.

Timeline of Jackie Chan's Life

1954 — Jackie Chan is born on Victoria Peak in Hong Kong, on April 7

1961 — Enrolls in the China Drama Academy in Kowloon, Hong Kong

1971 — Graduates from the China Drama Academy and begins movie work as a junior stuntman for Shaw Brothers Studio

1973 — Does stunt work on Bruce Lee's film *Enter the Dragon*

— Bruce Lee dies unexpectedly

1976 — Plays lead in Lo Wei's remake of *Fist of Fury* called *New Fist of Fury* in Hong Kong

1978 — Stars in *Drunken Master*

— Acts in and directs *The Fearless Hyena*

1980 — Acts in *The Big Brawl* in the United States

— Badly injured filming *Armour of God* in Yugoslavia

1995 — Stars in *Rumble in the Bronx* and receives MTV Lifetime Achievement Award

1998 — Costars with Chris Tucker in *Rush Hour,* making Jackie an international star

2002 — Receives star on the Hollywood Walk of Fame

2010 — Costars with Jaden Smith in a remake of *The Karate Kid*

2016 — Receives an Honorary Oscar Award for lifetime achievement

2017 — Stars in *The Foreigner*

Timeline of the World

1955	Ray Kroc opens his first McDonald's fast-food restaurant on April 15 in Des Plaines, Illinois
1963	President John F. Kennedy is assassinated in Dallas, Texas, on November 22
1968	Dr. Martin Luther King Jr. is assassinated in Memphis, Tennessee, on April 4
1969	Neil Armstrong walks on the moon on July 20
1981	Sandra Day O'Connor becomes first woman on the US Supreme Court
1988	Wrigley Field in Chicago, Illinois, becomes the last Major League Baseball park to add lights for night games
1991	The World Wide Web debuts as a public Internet service
2001	Al-Qaeda terrorists attack the United States in New York, near Washington, DC, and in Pennsylvania
2003	Space shuttle *Columbia* breaks apart upon reentry to the earth's atmosphere
2007	Nancy Pelosi becomes the first female speaker of the US House of Representatives
2008	Barack Obama is elected the first African American president of the United States
2010	Earthquake in Haiti becomes one of the worst natural disasters on record
2018	The Hong Kong–Zhuhai–Macau Bridge, the world's longest sea-crossing bridge, opens in China

Bibliography

*Books for young readers

Chan, Jackie. *I Am Jackie Chan: My Life in Action*. New York: Ballantine, 1999.

Corcoran, John. *The Unauthorized Jackie Chan Encyclopedia: From* Project A *to* Shanghai Noon *and Beyond*. New York: McGraw-Hill, 2003.

Gentry, Clyde. *Jackie Chan: Inside the Dragon*. Dallas, TX: Taylor Trade Publishing, 1997.

*Gifford, Clive. *Martial Arts Legends*. New York: Crabtree Publishing Co., 2009.

Greene, David. "Jackie Chan Jumps Back into the Action With 'The Foreigner,'" *NPR*, October 13, 2017, www.npr.org/2017/10/13/557166099/jackie-chan-jumps-back-into-the-action-with-the-foreigner.

*Poolos, Jamie. *Jackie Chan*. New York: Rosen Publishing Group, 2002.

Websites

www.jackiechan.com